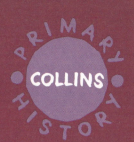

GW01319813

Victorian Britain

Grant Bage

Contents

Introduction

Queen Victoria was the queen of Britain from 1837 to 1901. She had a family of nine children. **Historians** find out about people in the past. Like detectives, they use clues called **evidence** in their work. Often they disagree about what the evidence means. This is what two historians have written about Queen Victoria and her family:

Historian 1

Above all it seems clear that Victoria hated pregnancy, hated childbirth, hated babies and hated children.

Historian 2

All the fun which Victoria had missed as a child she now had with her children: games of blind man's buff, visits to the zoo, on wet days games and scenes from plays.

If you only had the picture on the opposite page as evidence about Queen Victoria and her family, would you think that she enjoyed having a family, or not?

The royal family was just one of millions of families in Britain between 1837 and 1901. This period is known as the Victorian age, but how was Victorian life different from how we live today?

▲ Queen Victoria and her family in 1846.

We want *you* to find out. Become a historian: use the many different pieces of evidence in this book to answer questions and to ask some of your own. Warm up with this quiz!

True or false? For most of Victorian times,

a Most 11-year-olds did not have to go to school.

b Cars were unknown.

c Football was a popular sport.

d There was no electricity in houses.

e Over half the people lived in towns or cities.

f You could post a letter to anywhere in Britain for a penny.

g Many children died when they were very young.

h Clothes were fastened by buttons.

i Women could not vote.

Homes

Victorian Britain had millions more people than ever before, so new houses had to be built. These extra people lived mostly in the growing towns or cities. The graph shows just how fast the **population** was increasing.

Our towns and cities still contain Victorian buildings, but how can you tell when you are looking at one?

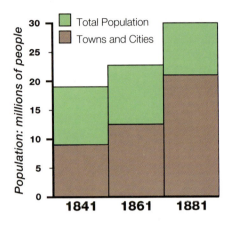

Legend:
- Total Population
- Towns and Cities

Y-axis: Population: millions of people (0, 5, 10, 15, 20, 25, 30)
X-axis: 1841, 1861, 1881

The outside

▲ Terrace of workers' cottages in Bolton, Lancashire. Terraced houses were common.

▶ Victorian three-storey houses. Red bricks were often used by Victorian builders.

In these pictures you can find clues as to whether a building or area is Victorian. They show some of the Victorian 'fashions' liked by the rich and poor. Check the houses in your neighbourhood for the same **features** to tell whether they were built in Victorian times.

▲ A date sign on the end wall of a row of Victorian houses.

▲ A Victorian pillar box. What do the initials VR stand for?

► Railings were multi-coloured until Prince Albert died. Then Queen Victoria started a new fashion by having them painted black.

▼ A Victorian window with panes of glass separated by lead.

Often the better houses were in **suburbs** on the edge of towns where there was more space to build.

▶ A suburban Victorian street in Fulham.

Mablethorpe Road, Fulham, S.W.

The houses built for the workers were small and cramped; living conditions could easily become dirty and unhealthy.

▼ A view from a train of London streets in Victorian times.

A Victorian wrote this about Manchester in 1844:

In a curve of the river surrounded by tall factories, high banks and buildings, stand about 200 back-to-back cottages in which live about 4000 Irish. The cottages are old, dirty and of the smallest sort, the streets in part without drains or pavements. Masses of refuse and filth lie every where in pools; the air is poisoned by these and darkened by the smoke of a dozen tall factory chimneys.

The inside

This was a Manchester factory worker's house in 1862. Poor people usually had few rooms and did not own much furniture.

▲ A factory worker's room.

Some rich people, like Charles Booth (a Liverpool shipowner), worked to make things better. They wrote about what they saw. This house was in a London street:

On the second floor live Mr and Mrs Park with five children. The man served in India as a soldier and left in ill-health. The mother works hard for her children. The room was full of rubbish, the dirty walls covered with little pictures never taken down. Rats were everywhere and the smell was awful. These people did have seven children but two of them, aged nine and eleven, disappeared going to school one morning and have never been heard of since.

Many Victorian houses were much more comfortable. The rooms were full of furniture and decorations. They looked very cluttered.

▲ A painting of the hall and staircase of a country house.

▶ A museum reconstruction of a mid-Victorian dining-room.

◪ **a** Victorian towns grew faster than the population in the countryside. Can you find out why from this book?

b List the reasons for and against moving into a Victorian city like Manchester.

c Can you find a street near you with Victorian features like the ones on pages 4 to 5? Sketch the features. How do they help us find out about Victorian life? What do they tell us?

d Look at rooms on this page. How are these the same as rooms in your house? How are they different? What is missing that might be in a modern room?

⚠ **a** In Victorian times streets were often named after famous people or events. Find and research some near you.

Families

Families were larger than nowadays. Having several brothers or sisters was common. Remember that Queen Victoria had nine children.

We can find out about local Victorians by using the **census**. This is a list made every ten years which tells us people's ages, names, jobs, family sizes and addresses. We still have a census today: the last one was in 1991.

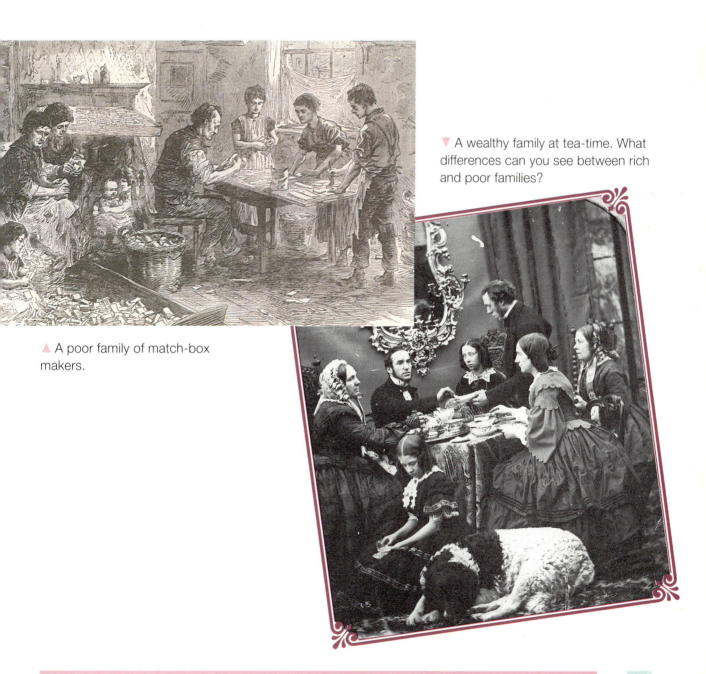

▼ A wealthy family at tea-time. What differences can you see between rich and poor families?

▲ A poor family of match-box makers.

Rich families

Young Florence Nightingale, a girl from a wealthy family, wanted to go out to work. Her family wanted her to be the same as their friends' daughters: to get married, have children and look after the house. Florence wrote this:

> Oh, evenings that never seem to draw to an end - for how many years have I watched that drawing room clock and thought it would never reach ten! And for 20, 30 years more to do this! Women don't think of themselves as human. There is no work for them at all except for looking after the family.

Find out what happened to Florence on page 12.

Wives worked hard for their families, but husbands had the last say. Mrs Beeton wrote a famous 'Housekeeping Book' for young wives like herself. This is her advice for breakfast-time:

> As soon as you hear your husband's step the bell should be rung for the hot dish; and should he be rather pressed for time, you yourself should wait upon him, cutting his bread, buttering his toast etc. Also give orders that coat, hat and umbrella should be brushed and ready.

Rich families paid servants called nannies to help with their children. This man remembers his childhood in Yorkshire in the 1890s:

> She [the nanny] taught us to read and write, she nursed us, she looked after us. If the truth be told I had perhaps more affection for my nanny than I had for my mother because she treated me almost as her own child.

Governesses were another kind of servant. They taught richer children at home.

A painting from 1844 of a governess. Does she look happy?

Boys and girls from poor families might find work as servants or **domestics** for richer families. Wages were low, but they were fed and housed in return for their work. Servants had strict ideas about how they did their work. The oldest and most experienced servants got the best jobs and were in charge of the others. The servants did the washing, cleaning and cooking in a household. They might also be gardeners, butlers or grooms.

A group of domestics working for a Victorian family.

Florence Nightingale

This is the story of a famous and unusual Victorian. She was born in 1820, whilst her rich parents were on holiday in a city called Florence.

She did not want to be like other girls and marry a rich man. She wanted to work as a nurse. Victorian people did not think much of nurses. Most nurses could not read or write and hospitals were often filthy places where people were left to die. No rich woman in her right mind would work in one... but Florence wanted to. Her parents hoped she would grow out of it and kept inviting handsome young men around. One waited for seven years because he loved her so much - but she still would not marry him!

She had nearly given up hope of nursing when by chance she met a man called Sidney Herbert. Through him and his wife, Florence at last found work - running a hospital for poor people in London.

She was not at the hospital for long when a war started in 1854, far away by the Black Sea. News came through that even when battles were won, sick or wounded soldiers were dying in great pain. Within weeks Florence set off with a small group of 38 women to nurse the soldiers. Everything was a mess, and the men in charge did not seem to care. Using her own money and stories in the *Times* newspaper, she stirred up a fuss. Fresh air, proper toilets and better food were brought to hospitals. Florence was unstoppable: one day she even killed a rat with her parasol! The ordinary soldiers loved her as 'the lady with the lamp', even though many of their officers hated her as a bossy woman. But she became the nation's heroine.

The first of many nurse-training schools opened in London in 1860. By the time Florence died in 1910, ideas about hospitals and nurses had changed completely.

Poor families

Life for factory workers was very different, especially at the start of Victorian times. Many mothers worked. Sometimes a woman would return to the factory only two or three days after giving birth and she could not take the baby with her. When there was a break she had to rush home to feed the baby and get her own meal. Can you guess who looked after the baby if both parents could not?

In poor city areas this was a common sight:

At the open door sits a girl of eight, a typical 'little mother' of the London doorsteps. She nurses a heavy baby, perhaps a year old. She talks to it, soothes it, hushes it to sleep, rocks it and kisses its poor little face again and again. But every other minute she has to look to a sister aged four and a brother aged five. Because she is the oldest all that come after are hers to tend and watch.

▼ A London slum. Look carefully at the clothes these Victorians are wearing.

Children often looked after each other in groups, like this one photographed in London.

Children played out in the street much more than now. Once indoors, children had to behave themselves. In strict homes they were expected to be 'seen and not heard'. Fathers would fix the evenings when older children (especially girls) could go out and wanted to know where they were and who they were with. They also set the time for their return; few dared break the rule. One girl of nineteen was beaten for coming home ten minutes late after choir practice.

Life for poor people living in the country could also be hard. This Wiltshire woman was interviewed in 1843.

I have had thirteen children, and brought seven up. I have been used to work in the fields at hay-time and harvest. Sometimes I have had my mother or sister to take care of the children. I have gone to work at seven in the morning till six in the evening. In making hay I have been strained with the work so bad sometimes I could not get out of my chair.

◑ **a** Families today tend to have fewer children. Why were Victorian families so large?

◪ **a** Act out a scene of master and servants in Victorian times. Make sure everyone gets a fair chance to play the different roles.

b Look at the rooms on page 8. Imagine that you were a servant and had to clean them. How many different tools and materials would you use? Find out which ones the Victorians would have had.

School

Most children in the past did not have to go to school. Rich people sent children, especially boys, away to school, or paid teachers to come to their homes. Before Victorian times there were few full-time schools for ordinary children.

Children who were already working were taught to read at Sunday schools. In 1833 the government started giving churches money to build more day schools. By 1870 half of six to ten-year-olds went to school. Children often worked to support their families and parents could not afford to lose their wages. However, business people and leaders were worried. If Britons could not read and write would the country stay rich and strong? As more men were allowed to vote they needed educating to use their vote well. Women could not vote in Victorian times.

In 1870, a law was passed to build more schools. All children between five and thirteen could go to school if they paid. It was 1880 before all under ten-year-olds *had* to go to school. Free education for all started in 1891.

▼ A school in 1839 where the older children are acting as teachers.

1839

▶ The inside of a village school in 1846. List the objects and say what they were used for.

Schools did not have much furniture. The writing desks had shelves where children could put books. The desks were put in rows facing the front of the room.

Most schools were very strict. This is how one class had to leave lessons in the 1870s:

All the children in a class came out in order to a series of commands. One! and you stood in your desk. Two! and you put your left leg over the seat. Three! and the right joined it. Four! you faced the lane between the classes. Five! you marched on the spot. Six! you stepped forward and the pupil-teacher chanted, 'Left, right, left, right.' It was agony, you were so longing to get outside. But if one boy pushed another you would have to go back and begin again.

But there were playtimes, and most schools from poor **workhouses** to richer boarding schools let boys play sports.

▶ Rugby school in 1870. What is going on in the picture?

Classrooms were often big as sometimes there were seventy or eighty pupils in a class. There could be more than one class in a room. Here is a picture of a London classroom in 1889.

▼ How many children are there in this classroom?

Victorian lessons were mainly the three 'R's' of reading, writing and arithmetic. There were also lessons where boys and girls were split into groups. Whilst the boys learned book-keeping, the girls would be learning needlework. Object lessons were popular. These were talks by teachers on topics like bread, coal or a postage stamp. The children had to listen carefully and, at the end of the talk, remember what had been said and repeat it to the teacher. They usually had to draw pictures of the object.

Here is a lesson timetable for a boys' school in Leeds at the end of Queen Victoria's reign.

▼ A school timetable.

Time	Standards IV V VI	Standard III	Standard II	Standard I
9·0 – 9·15	Opening of School Bible Lessons			
9·15 – 9·40	Hear Home Lessons and mark Registers			
9·40 – 10·0			Reading	Writing
10·0 – 10·30	Dictation or Arithmetic	Dictation	Arithmetic	Reading
10·30 – 11·0	Reading or Transcription	Arithmetic		
11·0 – 11·15	Playground			
11·15 – 12·0	Arithmetic	Reading	Transcription	Arithmetic
2·0 – 2·30		Writing	Arithmetic	Reading
2·30 – 3·0	Dictation or Arithmetic	Arithmetic	Reading	Letters & Figures
3·0 – 3·30	Reading or Transcription	Reading	Writing	Counting
3·30 – 3·45	Playground			
3·45 – 4·25	Object Lesson	Grammar	Transcription	Writing
4·25	Give out Home Lessons			
	Pupil Teachers			
1·0 – 2·0				

▲ Truants in 1859 playing marbles.

Some children and their parents disliked school. A school inspector wrote in 1884:

You find a group of children in the street playing at marbles, during school hours. 'Why are you not at school today?', 'Mother sent me for a bit of coal sir' or, 'Mother's gone out and I stayed to watch the baby' or, 'Please Sir, mother wanted me'. It seems every errand, in the mother's eyes, is more important than for her child to be late or absent from school.

◑ **a** Imagine you are the parent of a Victorian child who did not want to go to school. Persuade him or her to go with as many reasons as you can.

◩ **a** Use the evidence in this chapter to compare Victorian classrooms to your own. How have classrooms changed?

b Using the evidence from this chapter, write out a Victorian timetable for your class.

▲ **a** Find out the kinds of needlework that Victorian girls used to do. Design an embroidery to show what life was like in a Victorian school.

b Find out about the oldest school buildings in your area. Is there any evidence that they might be Victorian?

Spare Time and Money

As people became better off they had more spare time and money. They spent what they could afford on having fun.

The growth of the railways in Victorian times meant that people could move around the country more than before. Ordinary families could afford to visit the seaside. This was Ramsgate in 1854.

▲ Ramsgate Sands.

Charlotte Brontë was a famous Victorian writer who lived in Yorkshire. She once took the train to Bridlington in 1839. There were so many people on the pier they had to walk around in groups to make space. She wrote:

The idea of seeing the sea, of being near it, watching its changes by sunrise, sunset, moonlight and noonday, in calm and perhaps in storm fills my mind.

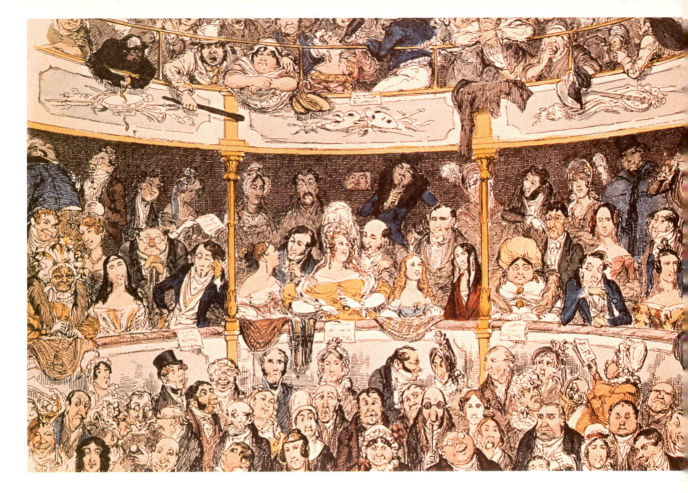

▲ A Victorian theatre audience.

Another treat was a visit to the theatre or to see **music-hall**. Famous performers included Sarah Bernhardt, Lillie Langtry and Marie Lloyd.

London children had their own version of the music hall. A journalist wrote:

It is a kind of theatre (admission one penny) where dancing and singing take place every night. The visitors are boys and mostly girls from eight to twenty: some of the girls, mere children, were dressed in showy cotton-velvet dresses and wore feathers in their bonnets. They stood laughing and joking with the lads. Singing and dancing were the whole of the hour's performance. A young girl of about fourteen danced with more energy than grace for the spectators who cheered her on by her Christian name.

Victorians loved music. In most towns, popular songs were played on a mobile barrel organ out in the street.

Like today, love songs were popular. This one has a clue to another Victorian hobby. What is it?

I will stand by you in wheel or woe,
        Daisy, Daisy,
You'll be the bell(e) which I'll ring, you know!
        Sweet little Daisy Bell!
You'll take the lead in each trip we take, then
        if I don't do well;
I will permit you to use the brake, my
        beautiful Daisy Bell!

▲ The organ-grinder often had a monkey to collect money from passers-by.

Many children made their own simple toys. Only those from well-off families had many bought toys. By 1900, toys were becoming cheaper so more children bought them.

◄ Ballroom dancers.

► Collection of miniature toys.

▼ Playing a game like billiards called bagatelle.

Cheap food and drink were also popular. This was London in 1872:

▼ Home-made ice-cream sold in a city street.

Wherever we travelled in crowded places we found the penny ice-man doing a brisk trade, even when his little customers were blue with cold. The ice-seller is the rival of the ginger-beer seller.

◧ **a** Look at the evidence on page 20. Make a list of the clothes being worn. Now do the same for a modern beach. How different are your two lists?

b Write and draw a postcard to a friend from a Victorian day out at the seaside.

c From the evidence, write what Victorians did in their spare time. Do the same for today. How and why have things changed?

△ **a** Charlotte Brontë was one of three sisters who were all famous Victorian writers. Find out more about their lives and their books.

b Learn a Victorian song and perform it. Ask your teacher for help.

Work

At the beginning of Victorian times, many women and children worked long hours down mines, in factories and up chimneys as sweepers.

▶ Children working down a coal mine.

▶ Children working in a cotton factory.

One girl talked about her job, sweeping horse manure from street crossings:

I'm twelve years old. Father's working so since mother's been dead, I've minded my little brother and sister and haven't been to school. When I goes a crossing-sweeping I takes them with me, and they sits on the steps close by. If it's wet I has to stop at home. Sister's three year old, and brother's five year old so he's just beginning to help me, sir. I hope he'll get something better than a crossing when he grows up. I used to go singing songs in the street but the songs grew so stale people wouldn't listen to them any more and as I can't read, I couldn't learn any more, sir.

People disagreed about how safe the new factories were where children worked. This man visited some factories in 1842:

The working rooms are high, spacious, and clean. There is nothing in sight, sound, or smell to offend. Great care had been taken with the 'boxing up' of dangerous machines. I learned that accidents were very rare.

A Scottish child remembered differently ten years later:

When I went to a spinning mill I was about seven. The whole was strange to me. The dust, the hissing and roaring, the bad language. One poor boy sat down to rest. In moments he was fast asleep. The master happened to pass. Without warning he gave him a violent slap, which stunned him. Half-asleep he ran to the machine and in five minutes his left hand got tangled with the machinery. Two of his fingers were crushed to a jelly.

Novelists like Charles Dickens showed how hard some women and children's lives were, and people joined groups which argued for improvements.

Gradually, governments made laws to help women and children working in mines and cotton factories. Here are some of the new laws that were made.

1825	Factory Act for cotton mills – 12-hour day maximum for children.
1842	Women banned from working underground in mines.
1844	Dangerous machinery had to be boxed in.
1850/53	Factory Acts – no more 60-hour working weeks for children in steam driven factories.
1867	Factory Act – children under 8 not to have a job in any workshop. 8-13 year olds to work no more than 30 hours a week, plus at least 15 hours school.

Conditions started to improve. Breaks from work became law.

▶ A painting of a factory workers' dinner hour.

People like Earl Shaftesbury and Dr Barnado argued for better treatment of children. Charities like the Shaftesbury Society and Dr Barnados were set up.

Industry

Mines, factories and new inventions changed how people lived and worked. This change is called the **Industrial Revolution**. It all started in Britain in the late 1700s and by Victorian times Britain had become the richest country in the world. Many people's standard of living rose.

New factories and machines needed power. At first this came from water and then from steam engines, heated by coal. The new workplaces were exciting and colourful as well as dangerous.

▶ The forge at Lymington Iron Works in 1832.

People still disagree about who gained from these new industries. Did they give the workers food, as this man claimed in 1844?

> We have seen children dying from sheer hunger in the mud-hovel, or in the ditch by the wayside. We would rather see boys and girls earning in the mill than starving by the road-side, shivering on the pavement or in prison.

Or was the truth nearer to the cartoon from 1843 on the bottom of page 28?

▶ What types of work can you see being done in this picture?

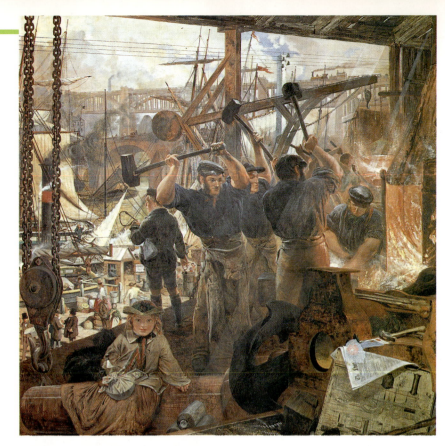

▼ A cartoon from *Punch* magazine.

Trades Unions

Workers formed groups called Trades Unions. They forced the government and businesses to make their working conditions better. This was not an easy thing to do. In 1834, a group of farm workers called the Tolpuddle martyrs were sent away to Australia for trying to raise their wages.

Trades Unionists had songs like this,

> They used to treat him as they liked in evil days of old,
> They thought there was no power on earth to beat the power of gold;
> They used to threaten what they'd do whenever work was slack,
> But now he laughs their threats to scorn with the Union at his back.

▲ A Trades Union certificate.

◑ **a** Use the evidence in this chapter to plan a TV programme about whether Victorian children should work or not. Act out parts of it.

b Compare the evidence about the conditions of work for Victorian children on page 25. Which accounts do you believe most and why?

c Look at the cartoon on page 28. What is it trying to show? Does it succeed?

◪ **a** Read through the book, listing all the different types of jobs that people did in Victorian times. How do they compare to jobs that people do today?

b Design a poster to convince Victorians that child labour should be abolished.

◭ **a** Research the stories of Earl Shaftesbury or Dr Barnado.

Out of Work

When they could not work through old age or sickness, Victorians could not expect a **pension**, unemployment or sick pay. Family, friends, or charities did what they could. Many charities were run by churches, some by working people in clubs.

Those needing help had to live in a special building called a workhouse, paid for by local taxes. This was made law in 1834. Workhouses were meant to be harsh enough to keep out those who could work, but soft enough to look after those who deserved it. They were very unpopular.

▼ What are the people in this workhouse doing?

Oliver Twist is a famous Victorian story by Charles Dickens. Oliver lives in a workhouse at the start of the book:

The evening arrived, the boys took their places. The gruel was served out and disappeared. Oliver was desperate with hunger. He rose from the table, and advancing to the master, basin and spoon in hand, said,

'Please sir, I want some more.'

The master was a fat, healthy man but he turned very pale.

'What!'

'Please sir,' replied Oliver, 'I want some more.'

The master aimed a blow at Oliver's head with the ladle and shrieked aloud for the Beadle.

a Do you think that workhouses were a good idea?

b Are stories by Victorian writers a fair way of finding out about life in Victorian times?

a Draw a picture to illustrate the scene from *Oliver Twist*.

a Look at the photograph of the workhouse on page 30 and find out more about what they were like.

Transport

Victorian cities had terrible traffic jams and pollution caused by horses. Horses were used to pull carts, waggons and buses. But people wanted to travel more easily and quickly.

▲ Ludgate Circus in 1877.

One of the best known engineers who improved transport in Victorian times was Isambard Kingdom Brunel.

A Victorian Engineer

Isambard Kingdom Brunel went to school in Brighton. The young boy made his friends laugh when he boasted how he could tell that a new building by the school was unsafe: but a few days later it fell down! After college, Isambard helped his father in the family engineering business. They built tunnels, docks and bridges but Brunel's biggest achievement was done alone - the "Great Western Railway".

This started in 1833. Tunnels and bridges appeared with amazing speed as the iron rails spread from Bristol to London. Every day brought problems to solve, but Brunel loved it because railways were so new and exciting. To build one bridge he laid an iron bar 300 metres long from one side to the other of a steep valley. Brunel was first across, hanging from the bar in a little basket!

Brunel had to be in charge and could be very strict. He told one worker, "You are a cursed, lazy, inattentive vagabond. If you continue to ignore my instructions and show such laziness I shall send you out!" Perhaps this was why it took only 5 years for the London-Bristol railway to be built.

Brunel wanted something new to think about. In 1852 he planned to build a metal ship using steam powered paddles and propellers, as well as sails. He wanted to sail it around the world. Five years later `The Great Eastern' was built but it got stuck when it was launched because it was so heavy. It was two months before it floated and the newspapers and crowds poked fun at Brunel. Finally, it went on its first voyage. Things went well ... but then an explosion shot one of the funnels into the air like a rocket, killing five sailors. Dare they tell Brunel the news? They did, and a few days later the great engineer died.

Railways

Railways were not popular at first because houses had to be flattened and the countryside spoiled to make room for them. Some stagecoach owners said these new railways were dangerous and unnatural. Eventually Victorians became very proud of their railways and built large, impressive railway stations.

► Which other forms of transport can you see in this photograph of Victoria Station?

The first trains were pulled by horses and had wooden rails. Richard Trevithick invented a small, moveable steam engine in 1802. It worked but was still too heavy on the light rails. The idea soon spread and rails were made stronger. By 1825 the first long railway was built between Stockton and Darlington. This was mainly for coal, with just a few

▼ Built in 1831, the Liverpool to Manchester railway soon carried more passengers than parcels.

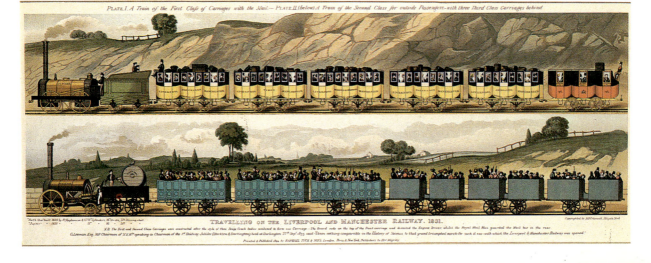

passengers. A bigger line was planned, from Liverpool to Manchester. Its owners held a competition for the best engine: the Stephenson's *Rocket* won it.

In 1837 this line was joined to Birmingham, and in 1839 to London. By 1850 there were over 5000 miles of railway track in Britain. This grew to 11 000 miles by 1865 and 18 000 miles by 1900.

▼ The British railway network in 1840 and in 1860.

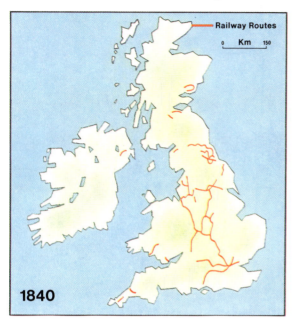

We have seen railways helping people to go on holiday (on page 20) but they also made it easier for people to travel for jobs. This was important. By using railways they found work in the towns. The painting on the front cover of this book shows all sorts of passengers on a train platform.

Other ways of travelling

Before the railways, express stagecoaches carried people to all parts of Britain. The railways killed this business off, but heavier goods like wood, coal or metal still went by waggon or canal boat. The canals were a very important way of transporting goods around Britain.

This painting shows Lincoln in 1858. It had a railway but looked like the seaside because of all the boats on the canal.

▶ Why was the canal so important to Lincoln?

Carts drawn by horses were still important right up until the end of Victorian times. The business in the photograph below was in London.

▼ What type of goods did this horse and cart carry?

▼ These sketches are from the 1870s. All the bicycles have something missing which modern bicycles use. What is it?

Bicycles became very popular. They were improved when the pump-up tyre was re-invented in 1888 by a Belfast vet.

The police have strict orders to arrest any Bicyclist riding without a bell or whistle

The DANDY of pre-historic times

The Bone-shaker of the middle ages

◖ **a** Why do you think the Victorians believed railways were so important? Do people still think this?

b Which do you think was the best form of Victorian transport and why?

◪ **a** Imagine that you have just travelled on the Liverpool to Manchester train, pulled along by Stephenson's *Rocket*. Write a letter about your journey.

b Look at the picture on page 34. Can you explain the differences in the carriages?

c Draw a time-line of when the main changes took place in railways.

d Choose some of the passengers in the painting on the front cover and write down what they might be saying or thinking.

▲ **a** Get a map of Britain that shows today's railways, from your local railway station. Are there more or less tracks than in Victorian times?

Towns and Cities

The biggest change in Victorian Britain was that for the first time most people lived in towns and cities (see the graph on page 4). Scottish, Welsh, Northern and Midland towns grew quickly. They were close to coal mines for power, and rivers and railways for transport.

▶ Stockport viaduct: railways and canals helped towns like Stockport to grow.

At first the changes were patchy. Parts of Manchester in 1849 were still like the countryside:

I climbed a roughly paved lane of mean houses, some of them little workshops. I heard on all sides the rattle of weaving machines. Still the look of the place was half country, trees here and there by the cottages. I was met by a decently dressed middle-aged woman. Her work-room had an earth floor, scratched by six hens jerking their heads about beneath the machinery of the four looms.

▼ The Manchester Royal Exchange was the place where three-quarters of Britain's cotton was sold.

Yet just 35 years later the Royal Exchange had been put up in the centre of Manchester.

The Victorians built impressive public buildings in towns and cities to show off their new wealth.

Great public parks were laid out to improve life in the cities.

Victorian Britain also had hundreds of small towns. County **directories** listed their shops and businesses, like telephone books today. There is probably a directory for your local area.

Bury St Edmunds in Suffolk had one in 1844, telling us that 12 500 people lived there. Stagecoaches left daily for London, Cambridge, Ipswich and Yarmouth. Carts came to its markets from 112 different villages.

A few of the businesses in the town are listed below.

▲ Bolton Town Hall shows grand Victorian architecture.

▲ Queen's Park in Glasgow was laid out in Victorian times.

	Total		Total
Bakers & Flour Dealers	45	Hairdressers	14
Bankers	5	Pawnbrokers	3
Blacksmiths	12	Staymakers	11
Boot & Shoemakers	68	Straw Hat Makers	20
Coachbuilders	8	Wheelwrights	7
Grocers & Tea Dealers	22	Whitesmiths	7

Ireland and its people

Unlike the rest of Britain, Ireland did not have many new industries and towns. Instead it had lots of small farms, rented by local people but owned by landlords far away. The farms were not well-run and the families on them were poor. There were few other jobs that they could do locally other than farming.

Potatoes were the main food, but in 1845-47 they caught a disease so there was little else to eat. 700 000 Irish people starved and a million left home. Many headed for the growing cities of the rest of Britain, like Liverpool and Glasgow.

▶ Irish settlers in London.

☑ **a** Look at a *Yellow Pages* or *Thomson's* directory. How have businesses in your town changed from the list on page 39?

b Use the evidence in this chapter to write a story about arriving in a Victorian city looking for work.

⚠ **a** Find a Victorian directory (Kellys) for your town in your nearest reference library. Look for a street which still exists today that appears in the directory. Draw a careful picture of the modern street and how it might have looked in Victorian times.

Public Health

We have all had a cold or tummy ache, and a few of us may have been to hospital. If we are ill, medical treatment is free and usually works. Yet hospitals, doctors and nurses as we have them now were new in Victorian times. Scientists were still discovering more about medicines. Many children died at birth, or before they grew up, of diseases that had no known cure.

Some Victorians knew that dirty water and poor housing led to diseases like cholera and typhoid.

▲ A cartoon called 'Court for King Chlorea'. What is causing cholera?

▶ A street in Glasgow. Can you see the water supply?

Public health was the answer. Plans for clean water, good food and warm houses were needed. Some towns had been built too quickly without strong sewers or a proper a water supply.

People like Edwin Chadwick, the campaigner for the poor, wanted piped water in 1842:

Fetching and carrying in buckets from wells does not do the job. The families in the factory towns rise early, before daylight in winter time, to go to work. They toil hard and return home late at night. It is difficult and uncomfortable to fetch water at a distance out of doors from the pump or the river in cold, rain and snow.

▼ The sewage from pigsties and toilets was emptied into rivers, like in this print of Jacob's Island in Bermondsey. River water was used for drinking.

▶ The cartoon of Father Thames and his children shows how this sewage spread disease. Who are his children?

In Burton-on-Trent poor families used only nine buckets of water each week. That was for a family of about five people and included washing clothes, cooking, cleaning, drinking and washing themselves. People began to realise that disease was caused by drinking water from rivers into which their toilets were emptied.

In 1848 the government made a 'Public Health' law because bad water was causing serious health problems. **Sewers** began to be built and efforts were made to make drinking water purer. Huge new reservoirs were made to supply drinking water and water for flushing toilets in the 1880s. By the end of the century, most town and city streets were being swept regularly to prevent the build-up of dirt and disease.

A favourite Victorian saying was 'Cleanliness is next to Godliness'. The success of scientists in discovering the reasons for certain diseases made the Victorians more aware of the need to keep themselves clean. People started to use soap in large amounts.

Medical breakthroughs were important in persuading Victorians to build more hospitals. Scientists

▲ A firm of public disinfectors with their equipment.

▶ A Pear's soap advertisement.

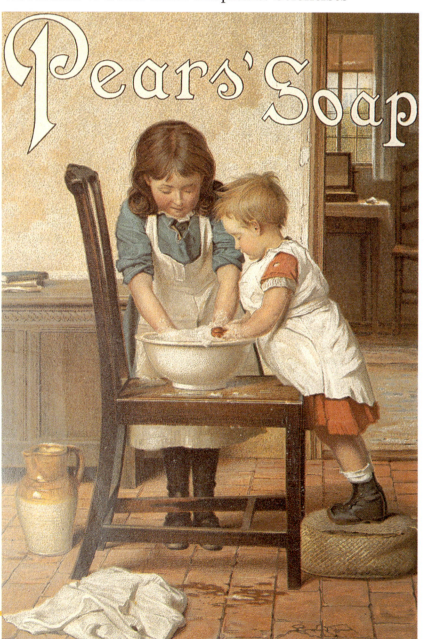

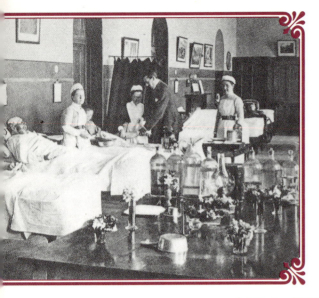

discovered that disease was caused by germs. This led to successful vaccines for preventing certain illnesses. Surgeons began to operate using gas that made patients unconscious to pain; and chemicals called antiseptics were invented to stop wounds from becoming infected. By the end of Victorian times, people had a better chance of fighting off diseases.

▲ A hospital ward in Aberdeen Royal Infirmary.

◑ **a** Did the Victorians improve health? Use the evidence from the chapters on homes, families and work to help you decide.

◪ **a** Write down and draw pictures of all the ways in which the Victorians tried to make people healthier. Put them in order of importance and be ready to explain the order you have chosen.

b Explain what the cartoon on page 42 is trying to show. Draw your own about another Victorian health problem.

▲ **a** Find out more about the improvements that the Victorians made in medicine.

b Investigate diseases like cholera and typhoid. Why do they still exist?

Shopping, Trade and Empire

At the same time as Victorians became wealthier, the price of goods became cheaper. Factories produced more goods than ever before. In 1872 this market trader explained:

> There really isn't any knowing what we shall come to. People want so many more things than they did when I was a lad.

▼ Victorian advertisements.

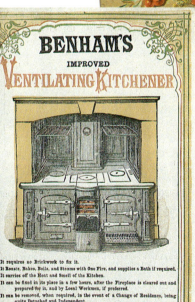

This growth in the number of goods happened because factories and railways brought things more cheaply to the towns. David Lewis, Jesse Boot and Thomas Lipton opened shops which still bear their names today.

Goods were sent to the shops and were traded. **Trade** means buying and selling, which Victorian Britain did more than most countries. By 1870 Britain was trading abroad as much as France, Germany and Italy put together, and four times as much as the USA. Part of this trade was with the **British Empire**, foreign lands which Britain controlled.

The British Empire

France, Germany and Britain all had empires made from foreign lands. Britain's was the biggest in the world.

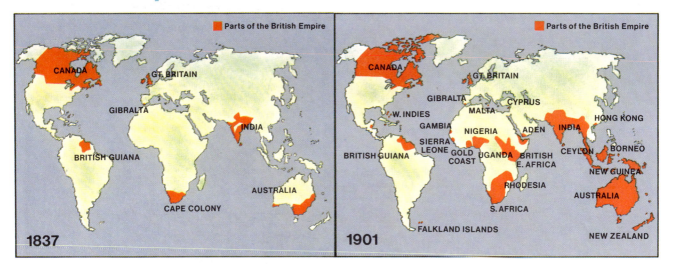

1837

CANADA
GT. BRITAIN
GIBRALTA
INDIA
BRITISH GUIANA
AUSTRALIA
CAPE COLONY

Parts of the British Empire

1901

CANADA
GT. BRITAIN
GIBRALTA
CYPRUS
MALTA
W. INDIES
HONG KONG
GAMBIA
NIGERIA
ADEN
INDIA
SIERRA LEONE
GOLD COAST
UGANDA
BRITISH E. AFRICA
CEYLON
BORNEO
BRITISH GUIANA
NEW GUINEA
RHODESIA
AUSTRALIA
S. AFRICA
FALKLAND ISLANDS
NEW ZEALAND

Parts of the British Empire

▲ The Empire on which the sun never sets.

Between 1853 and 1880, 2.5 million people left Britain or emigrated to live in the Empire or the USA. They believed their lives abroad would be much better.

▶ A cartoon on emigration.

HERE   AND   THERE;

Charles Kingsley, a famous children's author, wrote in 1873:

> Let me ask, are none of you going to emigrate? If you have courage and wisdom you will, instead of stopping here to scramble over each other's backs for the scraps, like black beetles in a kitchen.

Some of the countries liked being controlled by Britain, others did not. This could mean bloodshed as in the South African war of 1879 between the **Zulu** tribes and the British army. Gladstone, a Prime Minister in Victorian times, wrote:

> A nation who we call savages have in defence of their own land offered their naked bodies to the terrible cannons of modern science and have been mowed down, hundreds and thousands, having done bravely what were for them their duties.

▼ The Bombay Terminal railway station, in India, used to be named after Queen Victoria.

However, British rule left countries in the Empire with a new law system, impressive public buildings and railways. In India, the British had built 25 000 miles of railway by 1900. The British who ruled the Empire believed that using British ideas on law and business made these countries better places.

The Empire also meant lots of parades and celebrations at home. Queen Victoria was made Empress of India.

The chorus of a popular song from 1878 summed up British ideas. The Empire in India was threatened by a war with Russia:

> We don't want to fight but by jingo if we do –
> We've got the ships, we've got the men, and got the money too!

Parts of the old Empire remain, like the Falkland Islands and Hong Kong (until 1997). Most of it has been changed into the **Commonwealth** of Nations. It has regular meetings to talk about matters which affect all the member countries.

▲ A painting called 'Dreams of glory'. What is the little boy dreaming about?

◖ **a** Look at the cartoon on page 46. What did the artist wish to show?

b Look at the advertisements on page 45. What can we learn from them? Are advertisements useful for someone wanting to find out about the past?

◨ **a** Design an advert for the products on page 45 as if you were advertising it in a modern magazine.

b Find two different points of view in this chapter about the British ruling in foreign countries. Now decide what you think.

△ **a** Find out more about a country that used to be part of the British Empire. How did the country change by being part of the Empire?

Science and Technology

Victorians were famous for putting ideas into action, and Victorian Britain became 'the workshop of the world'. There was a Great Exhibition of wonderful new things made in Britain and the rest of the world. It happened in London in 1851. Queen Victoria's husband Prince Albert helped to organise it. Victoria was proud because it was a huge success.

People from all over the country travelled to it by train. They bought special railway tickets to travel cheaply to London during the six months that the exhibition lasted. Six million people visited the Great Exhibition and turned the event into a big party. Some factory owners even gave workers a day off and paid for their journey and admission.

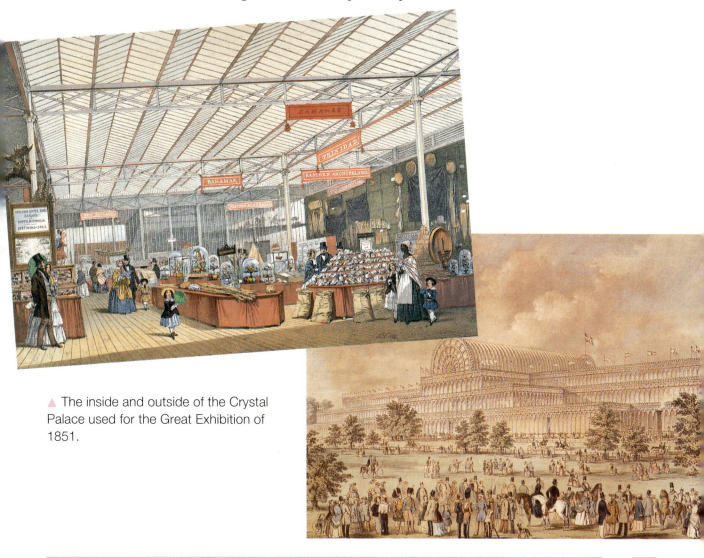

▲ The inside and outside of the Crystal Palace used for the Great Exhibition of 1851.

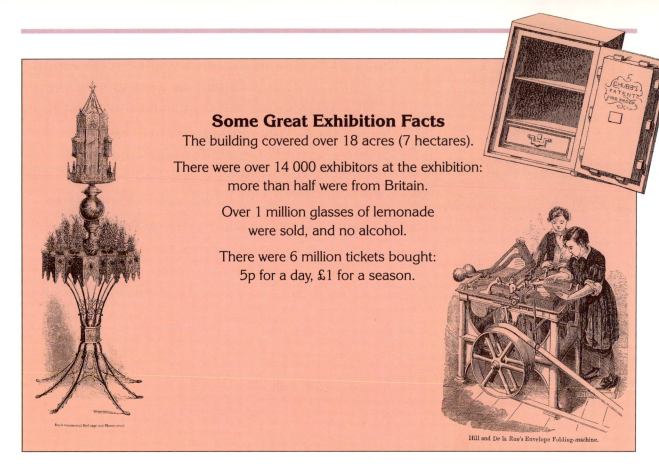

Some Great Exhibition Facts

The building covered over 18 acres (7 hectares).

There were over 14 000 exhibitors at the exhibition: more than half were from Britain.

Over 1 million glasses of lemonade were sold, and no alcohol.

There were 6 million tickets bought: 5p for a day, £1 for a season.

Rue's Ornamental Bird cage and Flower stand.

Hill and De la Rue's Envelope Folding-machine.

Steam engines

The Great Exhibition showed Victorian Britain at its best, but none of it would have been possible without steam engines for factories and railways. Steam power was used for fun as well.

▶ Fairground rides were steam-powered.

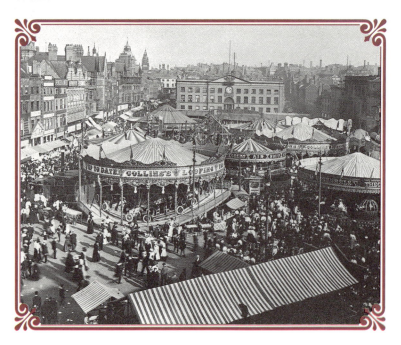

Photography

The first photographs were invented in Britain and France in the 1830s. People had to remain perfectly still for a long time for the photograph to be taken. This made them look rather grumpy! By 1871, most families had photographs on the mantlepiece:

▲ Holiday snaps!

Anyone who knows the lower classes has seen the spread of little portraits stuck over a labourer's fireplace: the boy gone to Canada, the girl out at service, the little one that sleeps under the daisies, old grandfather in the country. They will perhaps feel with me that the 6d photograph is doing more for the poor than all the charities in the world.

All the photographs in this book which have a border round them were taken in Victorian times.

Electricity

In the 1830s much was discovered about electricity, some of it in England by Michael Faraday. His ideas were important to the invention of **telegraphs** (Britain to America in 1866), the telephone (invented in Scotland in 1876), electric light (invented in 1879) and electric **trams** (first used in 1885 in Blackpool).

However even by 1900 electrical machines were not common. This washing machine went on sale in 1889.

◄ How is the machine powered?

Postage

◀ The first stamp: a penny black.

Before Victorian times, letters were sent by coach and by messengers that were not very reliable. The Victorians opened post offices to speed up the process. To pay for the improvements Rowland Hill invented stamps in 1840. The first stamps cost a penny each and showed Queen Victoria's head.

Evolution

Charles Darwin published new ideas in 1859 about where people and animals came from. He called this process **evolution** and it caused enormous arguments. He used science, fossils and animals to show that over time, creatures changed. This could mean that humans developed from apes a long time ago. This idea upset many Victorians who believed that God made humans starting with Adam and Eve. They thought that you could not believe in God and evolution at the same time.

a Every fifty years after the Great Exhibition, there is a special Trade Fair. When will the next one be? Design a poster for it showing possible exhibits.

b Choose a Victorian invention or discovery. Write down a list of the good and bad uses that people have made of the invention ever since.

c Look through the book at all the old Victorian photographs. How are they the same and how are they different from photographs taken today?

a Which ways of making power do we have that the Victorians did not have?

Religion

Church-going was very popular with Victorians. In 1851, six out of every ten people worshipped every week in Christian churches. How many do that in your class now?

The Victorians lavished care and attention on their churches. Over half of all the churches in Britain were restored and many new ones were built, mostly in towns and cities. Today nearly all churches have something Victorian in them, such as pews, altars or stained-glass windows.

Churches ran important charities. Life was hard for the poor and old, and governments helped less than now. This Norfolk vicar gave practical support:

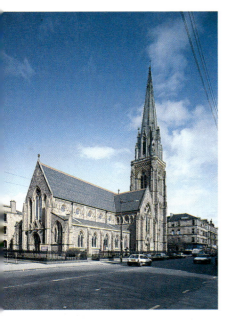

▲ St Mary's cathedral in Glasgow built in Victorian times.

▶ 'The Whit Walk'.

> Having said that I would give soup to any persons who would think it worth while to walk seven or eight miles in deep snow, I found today 33 at the door, to whom I gave from six to eight pints each.

Churches had a social side for children too, as in this Whit Sunday festival in Manchester.

Churches ran football or cricket clubs to encourage boys to go to church. Bolton Wanderers, Everton and Aston Villa are famous football clubs that grew in the 1870s, helped by churches or Sunday Schools.

New types of churches were started too, like the Salvation Army. It held lively services and helped orphans, the old and homeless. These children are queuing for a Salvation Army breakfast.

▼ These breakfasts cost a farthing. Find out how much money that is worth now.

a If you were building a new church in Victorian times, how would you attract people in? Design a poster showing your ideas.

b Go to your local church and draw the Victorian features you find in it.

a Research how the Salvation Army started. Has it changed much since Victorian times?

b Choose a charity to investigate. Did the charity start because of religion? How did the charity develop?

Glossary

British Empire Countries ruled directly by the British government.

census A special survey of everyone in Britain, done once every ten years. It records ages, jobs and addresses and is kept secret for one hundred years.

Commonwealth A group of countries, that used to be part of the British Empire.

directory A book of local information produced every year.

domestic A servant who worked inside a house.

evidence Something left from the past – includes writing, buildings, art. If we look at them carefully they can give us proof about the past.

evolution A theory that humans have developed from animals.

features Particular parts of a building, like doors, windows or decoration.

Industrial Revolution The name for the change by which Britain got most of its wealth from factories rather than from farming.

music-hall A type of theatre, popular in Victorian times, that is like a talent show.

pensions Money paid by the government to retired people who no longer work for a living.

population The number of people living in a place.

sewers Underground pipes that carry waste from toilets and drains to treatment factories.

suburbs The areas on the edge of a town or city where people live.

telegraphs Machines that send electrical signals over long distances.

trade The ways in which goods are bought and sold.

trams Electric buses that ran on tracks through city streets.

workhouse A place where people without jobs or money were sent.

Index

Acknowledgements

The publishers would like to thank the following for their permission to reproduce material:
Ancient Art and Architecture p4 (left). Bolton Metro p39 (top). Bridgeman Art pp8 (left), 16, 48 (top). BBC Radiovision Filmstrip 1974 p27. British Museum p21. Chester Toy Museum p22 (bottom x 3). Edifice/Lewis p5 (all photos). Mary Evans pp12, 22 (top), 24 (top), 30, 32, 33, 34 (bottom), 37, 51 (bottom). Geffrye Museum p8 (right). Stanley Gibbons Auctions Ltd p52. GLC p17 (bottom). Guthrie Photography p53 (top). Hammersmith and Fulham Public Libraries p6 (top right). Hulton Picture Company pp9 (right), 13, 15, 17 (top), 19, 34, 36 (bottom), 42 (left), 49 (both), 51 (top). Hutchinson Library p47. Ironbridge Gorge Museum p50 (top). Kensington Library p40. Manchester City Art Galleries p26. Manchester Public Libraries p53 (bottom). Mansell Collection pp6 (bottom left), 9 (middle), 41 (both). National Portrait Gallery p2. National Railway Museum p38 (top). National Trust p28 (top). Nottingham County Council p50 (bottom). Robert Opie Collection p45 (x 3). Punch pp28 (bottom), 42 (right). Radio Times Picture Library pp7, 24 (middle). Royal Collection pp30, 20. Royal Commonwealth Society Library p46 (bottom). Salvation Army p54. Smith/Thompson Collection 1875 from The Slide Centre, Illminster pp23, 43 (top). Spectrum Colour Library p38 (bottom). TUC p29. Unilever Historical Association p43 (bottom). Usher Gallery, Lincoln p36 (top). Victoria and Albert Museum p11 (top). Viewfinder p4 (right). George Young p39 (bottom).